SPOTLIGHT ON NATIONS

UNITED KINGDOM

JOE TISCHLER

CREATIVE EDUCATION · CREATIVE PAPERBACKS

Published by Creative Education and Creative Paperbacks
P.O. Box 227, Mankato, Minnesota 56002
Creative Education and Creative Paperbacks are imprints
of The Creative Company
www.thecreativecompany.us

Design and production by Graham Morgan
Art direction by Blue Design, Inc.
Edited by Ana Brauer

Photographs by Getty Images/BEN STANSALL, 27, Bettmann, 21, Grant Faint, 28, Sammyvision, 18, WPA Pool, 12; Pexels/Gene Taylor, 23, John Nail, 9, Kris Schulze, 16, Pixabay, 4–5; Unsplash/ Benjamin Davies, cover, 1, Dave Kim, 29, Sung Shin, 3; Wikimedia Commons/Arthur C. Michael, 11, Bonhams, 10, Conrad Martens, 15, Diliff, 24, Mod creator, 8, 10, 14, 16, 20, 22, public domain, 6, Robert Welch, 26, Yale Center for British Art, 17, Yousuf Karsh, 14

Every effort has been made to contact copyright holders for material reproduced in this book. Any omissions will be rectified in subsequent printings if notice is given to the publisher.

Copyright © 2026 Creative Education, Creative Paperbacks
International copyright reserved in all countries. No part of this book may be reproduced in any form without written permission from the publisher.

Library of Congress Cataloging-in-Publication Data
Names: Tischler, Joe author
Title: United Kingdom / by Joe Tischler.
Description: Mankato, Minnesota : Creative Education and Creative Paperbacks, [2026] | Series: Spotlight on nations | Includes bibliographical references and index. | Audience: Ages 10-13 | Audience: Grades 4-6 | Summary: "Explore the United Kingdom's rich history, popular landmarks, cultural heritage, government, and economy, plus its role in global politics and international organizations. Written for middle-grade readers, this book includes timelines, sidebars, glossary, resources, and index"-- Provided by publisher.
Identifiers: LCCN 2025018214 (print) | LCCN 2025018215 (ebook) | ISBN 9798895810750 library binding | ISBN 9798896800286 paperback | ISBN 9798895812013 ebook
Subjects: LCSH: Great Britain--History | England--Civilization | Scotland--History | Ireland--History | Wales--History
Classification: LCC DA32 .T57 2026 (print) | LCC DA32 (ebook) | DDC 941--dc23/eng/20250715
LC record available at https://lccn.loc.gov/2025018214
LC ebook record available at https://lccn.loc.gov/2025018215

Printed in the United States

CONTENTS

INTRODUCTION 4
Small County, Big Traditions

HISTORY 7
How the British Royal Family Began 8
Isaac Newton 10

GOVERNMENT 13
Winston Churchill 14
Brexit 16

PEOPLE, CULTURE, AND TRADITIONS 19
English Music 20
William Shakespeare 22

PLACE IN THE WORLD TODAY 25

All about the United Kingdom 29
Words to Know 30
Learn More 31
Index 32

INTRODUCTION
SMALL COUNTRY, BIG TRADITIONS

The United Kingdom (U.K.) is a group of islands in northwest Europe. It has been home to kings and queens, knights and castles, and some of the world's greatest inventors and writers. It is a land where the past and present come together in surprising ways. You can walk down a street where people lived hundreds of years ago, and just around the corner, you might find a busy city full of modern skyscrapers.

But what makes the U.K. so fascinating is the people and their incredible ideas. This is the country where William Shakespeare wrote his famous plays, where scientists such as Isaac Newton discovered life-changing things like gravity, and where the idea of a government "by the people, for the people" began to take shape. It's also a place full of **traditions**, like afternoon tea, driving on the left-hand side of the road, and celebrating the queen or king with grand parades.

There's also the beauty of its countryside, from the mysterious Stonehenge to the dramatic mountains of Scotland. Each part of the United Kingdom has its own **culture**, history, and stories to tell.

CLOSE-UP
Battle of Brunanburh

In 937, Athelstan led one of the most decisive battles in English history against a coalition of Scots, Vikings, and Britons. His victory secured England's existence as a unified nation.

CHAPTER ONE
HISTORY

The origins of the United Kingdom can be traced to the early 10th century. Anglo-Saxon king Athelstan conquered neighboring Celtic kingdoms. He declared himself "the king of all Britain." Later, in 1066, William the Conqueror took control of England and laid the foundation for a united kingdom. Over the following centuries, further wars gave the English more land.

Today, the U.K. consists of the countries of the island of Great Britain (England, Scotland, Wales) and Northern Ireland, which sits in the island of Ireland. The U.K. resides in Europe and is surrounded by the Atlantic Ocean, the North Sea, the English Channel, and the Irish Sea.

The official history of the U.K. begins in 1707, when the Treaty of Union was signed. The treaty united the Kingdoms of England and Scotland. The Acts of Union 1800 added the Kingdom of Ireland to create the United Kingdom of Great Britain and Ireland.

The Industrial Revolution (1760–1840) advanced industries such as shipbuilding, coal mining, steel production, and textiles. It transformed

MILESTONES IN THE UNITED KINGDOM'S HISTORY

4000 BC
▸ People start farming in the area. This is the start of the Neolithic Age or New Stone Age

43 AD
▸ The Romans invade, led by Emperor Claudius. They build roads and towns across England

economies and societies, paving the way for modern industrialization.

During its first 150 years, the U.K. was involved in many wars. The Seven Years' War began in 1756. By the end, it expanded the British empire at the expense of France. Britain lost 13 American colonies during the American Revolution (1765–83). The colonies formed the United States of America.

King George V (5) declared war on Germany and Austria in August of 1914, entering World War I (1914–18). The Royal Navy dominated the sea battles. The U.K. and its allies, which included France, Russia, Italy, and the U.S., won the war. The League of Nations was founded with the idea that nations could resolve their differences peacefully. Those dreams did not pan out.

CLOSE-UP
Windsor

Windsor Castle in Berkshire, England, is the oldest and largest occupied castle in the world. Built in the 11th century, it has been the home to the royal family for generations.

———— HISTORICAL  HIGHLIGHT ————

How the British Royal Family Began

The British Royal Family dates back to the early medieval period. Alfred the Great ruled the Kingdom of Wessex in the late ninth century. His grandson, Athelstan, was the first king of England. The modern royal family began in 1917 when King George V (5) created the House of Windsor. His son, Edward VIII (8) became king, but later gave reign to his brother, George VI (6). George VI's daughter, Queen Elizabeth II (2), began her 70-year reign in 1952. After her death in 2022, her oldest son, Charles III (3), became the King of the United Kingdom.

The U.K. was back at war with Germany in World War II (1939–45) following the German **invasion** of Poland. Britain and its allies came out victorious after the surrender of Germany and Japan.

Today, the armed forces of the U.K. are known as His Majesty's Armed Forces. His Majesty is the current king, Charles III (3). The U.K. has one of the most powerful armed forces in the world.

The U.K has a free market **economy**, where businesses operate with low taxes and few regulations. This is called the Anglo-Saxon model.

410
▸ The Romans leave. Celtic kingdoms reappear alongside Roman culture

449
▸ The Anglo-Saxons come. Christianity becomes popular nearly 150 years later

CLOSE-UP
Renaissance Man

Isaac Newton independently developed calculus, though German mathematician Gottfried Wilhelm Leibniz created a similar system around the same time. This led to a famous dispute. Newton also oversaw England's currency as Master of the Royal Mint, cracking down on counterfeiters.

─── HISTORICAL  HIGHLIGHT ───

Isaac Newton

Isaac Newton is one of the most important scientific figures in world history. Newton was born in Lincolnshire, England, in 1642. He developed the three laws of motion. The first law states that objects remain at rest unless acted on by unbalanced force. The second law states that force equals mass times acceleration. The third law states that for every action, there is an equal and opposite reaction. Newton also formulated the universal law of gravitation. This means the greater the mass of the objects, the stronger the force is between them.

The Magna Carta wrote that the **KING** was not above the law.

925
- King Athlestan is crowned. He is the first king of the area now known as England

1215
- The Magna Carta is signed by King John. It says the king must follow the rules of England. It also gives "free men" the right to a fair trial

CLOSE-UP
Royal Assent

Every bill passed by Parliament must be approved by the king or queen before it becomes a law. Today, this is mostly just a tradition. No monarch has said no to a bill since 1708.

CHAPTER TWO
GOVERNMENT

The royal family is an important part the United Kingdom, but they do not run the government. As of 2025, the **monarch** is King Charles III (3). The government is called "His Majesty's Government." The king is the head of state, but he does not make any political decisions. The **prime minister** is the real leader of the government. A general election is held every five years to choose a new a prime minister. The prime minister lives at 10 Downing Street in London. They lead the government and are the main leader in the House of Commons, which is the lower part of Parliament. The prime minister also picks other government leaders, including 22 cabinet ministers. These cabinet ministers make important decisions about the country.

The king has the power to appoint or dismiss a prime minister, although this has not been done since 1834. The king also commands the U.K.'s armed forces. He has the power to declare war and enact peace with other nations, but these decisions are usually made by the government.

Laws go through several stages before they are passed by Parliament. The House of Commons and the House of Lords work together to make them.

1337
▸ The Hundred Years' War begins. King Edward III of England tries to invade France. France wins

1348
▸ The bubonic plague kills nearly half of the population in one year

CLOSE-UP
Nobel Prize
Winston Churchill was awarded the Nobel Prize in Literature in 1953 for his historical writings and speeches.

— HISTORICAL  HIGHLIGHT —

Winston Churchill

Winston Churchill served two separate terms as prime minister of the United Kingdom (1940–45 and 1951–55). In a 2002 poll, he was voted the greatest Briton of all time. He is well remembered for his passionate, eloquent speeches. He led the U.K. to victory in World War II over Germany and he provided bold leadership during times of national crisis. Churchill died in 1965. He was given a state funeral, which is an honor normally saved only for kings and queens. A statue of Churchill stands in Parliament Square in London.

The U.K. has the sixth-largest economy in the world. Its **currency** is called the pound. England has the U.K.'s largest economy. It is followed by Scotland, Wales, and Northern Ireland. Tourism is a major industry. Nearly 40 million people visited the U.K. in 2024. London is the primary destination for foreign visitors. Buckingham Palace is one of the main sights to visit. The royal family lives there. The U.K. has many historic castles, museums, and theaters, which make it a popular tourist destination. Services, manufacturing, construction, and tourism contribute most to the U.K.'s economy.

Trade has long been a pivotal part of the U.K.'s economy. The U.K.'s biggest trade partners include the United States, Germany, and China. The nation imports about one-tenth of its food and about one-third of its machinery and transport equipment. The main exports include machinery, automobiles, electrical and electronic equipment, chemicals, and oil. London is also one of the world's top financial centers, where many banks and companies do business.

1559
▸ Queen Elizabeth I is crowned. She rules for 44 years

1642
▸ The English Civil War begins. King Charles I wants to go to war against Scotland, but Parliament does not support him. The conflict shifts to a struggle between King Charles I and Parliament

CLOSE-UP
Stonehenge

Stonehenge is located in England. It is one of the world's most famous prehistoric monuments. The first stones were placed around 3000 B.C. It is believed to have been built by several different groups over time.

──── HISTORICAL  HIGHLIGHT ────

Brexit

The European Union (EU) is a union of 27 European countries. In 2016, prime minister David Cameron called for a vote to decide if the U.K. should stay in the EU. He expected most people to vote to stay, but they voted to leave. In 2020, the U.K. became the first nation to officially leave the EU. Many believed the EU was not solving economic problems. The nation wanted to have more control over immigration, trade, and other issues. After the vote, Cameron resigned. Theresa May became prime minister but resigned in 2019. Brexit, or Britain's exit, was completed by the next prime minister, Boris Johnson.

The Great Fire of London destroys 80 percent of the city.

1666

- A fire starts in a bakery and destroys 80 percent of London. It is known as the Great Fire of London

1707

- The Treaty of Union between England and Scotland is signed. Great Britain is created

CLOSE-UP

Tea Time

Tea is a big part of life in the U.K. The British drink more than 163 million cups of tea a day. That's about 20 times more cups than people in the United States.

CHAPTER THREE
PEOPLE, CULTURE, AND TRADITIONS

British culture is a mix of ancient traditions and modern ideas. Centuries-old castles stand alongside cutting-edge architecture. History is the backbone of U.K. culture, and traditions are as varied as the regions of England, Scotland, Wales, and Northern Ireland.

The Roman conquest introduced Roman law, architecture, and roads. Roman merchants and settlers brought Christianity with them, which would become a cornerstone of U.K. culture. After the Romans withdrew, Anglo-Saxons invaded, bringing new languages and art forms. The Viking raids introduced Norse culture, further influencing the language.

Today, English is the most widely spoken language in the U.K. It is the nation's "unofficial" language. Other languages spoken in the region include Welsh, Scottish Gaelic, and Scots.

In the late 15th century, playwrights like William Shakespeare and Christopher Marlowe were part of the Renaissance movement. This movement encouraged curiosity and innovation.

1801
▸ Great Britain and Ireland join to form the United Kingdom

1914–18
▸ World War I brings social change as women join the workforce while the men are away

The British Empire influenced cultures worldwide. This made the U.K. a global power, in turn exposing it to a wide range of other cultures. The latter half of the 20th century and the early part of the 21st century have been characterized by social and technological change. This introduced a rich diversity of traditions, foods, and arts that have strongly influenced modern British culture.

There are many annual traditions throughout the U.K. Some involve grand royal ceremonies like the Trooping of the Colour, an event that marks the official birthday of the British monarchy. Northern Ireland celebrates Saint Patrick's Day every March 17, with parades, music, and the wearing of green.

Traditional attire varies across the U.K.'s regions. In Scotland, the kilt is the most iconic wear. It is a piece of clothing that looks like a knee-length skirt with heavy pleats, traditionally worn by men for special events or to express their heritage. In Wales, the traditional costume, often worn

English Music

The United Kingdom has many famous musicians. The Beatles, formed in Liverpool in 1960, are the bestselling music act of all time. Elton John, a singer, songwriter, and pianist, is one of only 21 people to win an EGOT. Singer-songwriter Adele has won 16 Grammy Awards and is from London. Queen, a legendary rock band from London, is known for its timeless songs. Other notable musicians include Snow Patrol, a rock band from Northern Ireland; Ed Sheeran, a singer-songwriter from Framlingham, England; and Marina, a pop star from Wales.

THE BEATLES

1939–45:

▸ The United States, Canada, and the U.K. join forces to fight Germany during World War II

1952

▸ Queen Elizabeth II (2) begins her reign. It lasts 70 years until her death in 2022. It is the longest reign of any British monarch

on Saint David's Day, includes a wool skirt, apron, and bonnet for women.

The U.K.'s traditional music includes a wide range of folk and classical forms. These include Scottish **bagpipes** and Welsh harp music. Folk music festivals are held throughout the U.K., celebrating this rich musical heritage.

CLOSE-UP
Cheese Rolling

Once a year, a cheese rolling competition down a steep hill takes place at Cooper's Hill in Gloucestershire, England. The winner takes home a wheel of cheese of their choice.

British food is known for its hearty and comforting dishes. Fish and chips are a popular meal in the U.K. It consists of battered and fried fish with thick-cut fried potatoes. Tea and scones are a significant part of British culture. Haggis is a traditional dish in Scotland. It is pudding that contains sheep organs encased inside the sheep's stomach.

HISTORICAL HIGHLIGHT

William Shakespeare

William Shakespeare is widely considered the greatest playwright of all time, as well the most influential writer in the history of the English language. He was born in Stratford-upon-Avon, England, in the 16th century. Five centuries later, his works are still performed on stages. One of his most famous plays is *Romeo and Juliet*. The musical *West Side Story* is a modern adaptation of his play. Other famous plays written by Shakespeare include *Much Ado About Nothing*, *King Lear*, *Othello*, and *Macbeth*.

Bagpipes are traditional MUSIC in the United Kingdom.

2016
- The UK votes to leave the EU. Their exit becomes official in 2020

2022
- Queen Elizabeth II (2)'s son Charles is crowned King following her death

CHAPTER FOUR
PLACE IN THE WORLD TODAY

The United Kingdom covers roughly the same area as the U.S. states of Minnesota and Iowa. Northern Ireland shares a land border with the Republic of Ireland. Great Britain is an island. Despite the U.K.'s northern location, the nation does not see much yearly snow due to its water borders.

The U.K. is a global power. It is a member of several international organizations. These include the United Nations Security Council, the G20, the G7, NATO, and the Council of Europe. The U.K. has a good relationship with the United States and a close partnership with France. The U.K. is also closely linked with the Republic of Ireland, with the two countries sharing a common travel area. Canada, Australia, and New Zealand are former colonies of the British Empire. They all share King Charles III (3) as their head of state.

Major sporting events are hosted in the United Kingdom. The most popular sport is soccer. The top league is the English Premier League (EPL). Some of the most popular teams are Manchester United, Chelsea, and Arsenal. Wimbledon is a Grand Slam tennis tournament held in London. It is the only one of the four Grand Slam events to be played on grass.

CLOSE-UP
The Titanic

The Titanic, the luxury ship that famously sank in 1912, was built in Belfast, Northern Ireland, in the early 20th century. Today, you can visit the Titanic Belfast museum to learn more about the ship's history.

London has hosted the summer Olympics three times, in 1908, 1948, and 2012.

Scotland is known as the "home of golf." The sport originated in the town of St. Andrews. The Royal and Ancient Golf Club of St. Andrews was founded in 1754. The Open Championship is often held there. It is one of golf's four major championships and the only one held outside the United States.

London is home to one of the "Big Four" fashion weeks. London Fashion Week takes place twice a year. More than 150 designers show off their best work across a series of catwalk shows. The British Museum is in London and is dedicated to human history, art, and culture. Its collection of eight million works is the largest in the world. Other parts of the U.K. also host major events. In Wales, the Eisteddfod is a festival that celebrates Welsh culture through literature and music. Northern Ireland hosts the Belfast International Arts Festival, an annual arts event featuring theater, dance, and music.

The United Kingdom has a rich history. The nation continues to shape culture, from the Royal Family to the Beatles and Shakespeare. Despite its small size, it is firmly established as a global power.

ALL ABOUT THE
UNITED KINGDOM

Continent: Europe

Capital: London, England

Population: 68 million

National language: English

Government: Unitary parliamentary, constitutional monarchy

Currency: Pound sterling

Main Religion: Christianity

Flag Colors: Red, white, blue

National Flower: Rose

WORDS to Know

bagpipes   a musical instrument with reed pipes that are sounded by the pressure of wind emitted from a bag squeezed by the player's arm

culture   the beliefs, social practices, and characteristics of a racial, religious, or social group

currency   standardization of money in any form

economy   the wealth or resources of a country or region

EGOT   the achievement of winning an Emmy, Grammy, Oscar, and Tony Award

invasion   act of entering a place, usually by force

monarch   a king or queen or is the official head of a country, often with limited or ceremonial powers

prime minister   the head of an elected government

tradition   customs or beliefs passed down from one generation to another

LEARN MORE

Books

Bolte, Mari. *King Charles III: Claiming the British Crown*. Minneapolis: Lerner Publications, 2023.

Gagne, Tammy. *Charles III: Kind of the United Kingdom*. Minneapolis: Core Library, an imprint of Abdo Publishing, 2025.

Walker, Tracy Sue. *Spotlight on the United Kingdom*. Minneapolis: Lerner Publications, 2024.

Websites

"UK Facts: United Kingdom." Kids World Travel Guide. https://www.kids-world-travel-guide.com/uk-facts.html

"United Kingdom." Britannica Kids. https://kids.britannica.com/kids/article/United-Kingdom/345811

"United Kingdom." National Geographic Kids. https://kids.nationalgeographic.com/geography/countries/article/united-kingdom

Documentaries

The Entire History of the United Kingdom. History. 2024. https://www.youtube.com/watch?v=l5vfL2NzVtaQ&t=128s

The Entire History of the British Monarchy. 4K Royal Family. 2024. https://www.youtube.com/watch?v=lIWHP7Jtyqzk

Wonders of the United Kingdom. The Most Amazing Places in UK – Travel Video 4K. 2024. https://www.youtube.com/watch?v=lTLR9mHULKJA

Note: Every effort has been made to ensure that any websites listed above were active at the time of publication. However, because of the nature of the Internet, it is impossible to guarantee that these sites will remain active indefinitely or that their contents will not be altered.

Visit

BUCKINGHAM PALACE

Visit one of the official residences of the Royal Family. The administrative headquarters of the Royal Family are here.

Buckingham Palace Road, London SW1A 1AA

BIG BEN
(GREAT CLOCK OF WESTMINSTER)

Visit one of the iconic landmarks of London. It is one of the most prominent symbols of the United Kingdom and parliamentary democracy.

Westminster, London SW1A 0AA, UK

OLD TRAFFORD

Visit the famous home stadium for the Manchester United English Premier League team. The team has been playing there since 1910.

Greater Manchester, England M16 0RA

STONEHENGE

Visit the iconic stone monument and follow the footsteps of the prehistoric people who lived here 4,000 years ago.

Salisbury SP4 7DE, UK

INDEX

Athelstan, 6, 7, 8

Brexit, 16, 23

Churchill, Winston, 14

King Charles III (3), 8, 9, 13, 15, 23, 25

monarchs, 4, 7, 11, 12, 13, 20, 21

music, 20, 22, 26

Newton, Isaac, 4, 10

Northern Ireland, 7, 15, 19, 20, 25, 26

prime ministers, 13, 14, 16

Queen Elizabeth II (2), 8, 15, 21, 23

Roman conquest, 9, 19

Scotland, 4, 7, 15, 17, 19, 20, 22, 26

Seven Years' War, 8

Shakespeare, William, 4, 19, 22, 26

soccer, 25

Stonehenge, 4, 16

tennis, 25

traditions, 4, 12, 19, 20, 22

Wales, 7, 15, 19, 20, 26

world wars, 8, 9, 14, 19, 21